My Body Is So Clever!

About Wise & Wide

- A systematic 6-level English reading program based on Lexile® measures
- Diverse and interesting topics chosen from the elementary curriculums of Korea and English speaking western countries
- Well-written books in various forms including fiction stories, descriptive texts, and classics retold
- The informative but original fiction stories grab your interest, leading to the easy and clear understanding of the educational content.
- Improve thinking skills with solid after-reading activities at all levels of the series.

Wise & Wide is a 6-level English reading program that consists of 60 books and each level is systematically divided by Lexile® measures. The Lexile® Framework for Reading is the most popular reading measuring system in American formal education curriculums and many English programs. Over 20 out of 50 states in the U.S. mark Lexile® measures directly on students' final report cards and over 300 well-known publishers adopt and use Lexile® measures.

Experience many kinds of readings written by professional writers from the U.S. and England. They used interesting topics that were carefully chosen after analyzing elementary curriculums from around the world including Korea, the U.S., England, and Australia among many others. Comprehensive after-reading activities including graphic organizers, speaking tasks, and After-reading Tests are ready for you.

Levels in the series and their corresponding Lexile® measures

Level	Lexile® measures	U.S. Grade
Level 1	Below 200L	Pre K - K
Level 2	190L - 400L	Lower Grade 1
Level 3	350L - 530L	Upper Grade 1
Level 4	420L - 650L	Grade 2
Level 5	520L - 940L	Grade 3 - 4
Level 6	830L - 1070L	Grade 5 - 6

* Smart Readers: Wise & Wide level 1 is applicable to the preschool level in the U.S.
* The source of the relationship between Lexile® measures and U.S. school grades: CCSS(Common Core State Standards) FOR ENGLISH LANGUAGE ARTS, APPENDIX A (2012, which is used by 45 states in the U.S.)

Topic List

	Level 1	Level 2	Level 3	Level 4	Level 5	Level 6
Book 1	Science>Biology: The hibernation of animals Story	Science>Biology: Living and nonliving things Story	Science>Biology> Animals & the Environment: Sea otters Story	Environment> Living with nature: The diver & the persimmon tree Story	Science>Biology> Animal: Amazing animals of the Amazon Story	Science>Biology: Germs, transmitted diseases Story
Book 2	Literature> World classics: Aesop's fables Story	Literature> Traditional fairy tale: Old tales about stones Story	Social Studies> Economy: To run a business to make and save money Story	Science>Biology> Plants: Photosynthesis Story	Science>Earth science: Earth's layers,earthquakes, volcanoes, and earth's atmosphere Report	Mathematics> Sequence: The golden ratio & the Fibonacci sequence Story
Book 3	Science>Physics: How shadows are formed Story	Literature> World classics: Peter Pan Story	Science>Scientific technology: Nanobots Story	Literature>Myths: World's creation stories Story	Literature> Legend: The story of King Arthur Story	Literature>Myths: Constellation myths Story
Book 4	Literature> Traditional literature: The Talmud Story	Science>Biology> Animal: Polar bears Story	Science>Biology> Animal: Mountain gorillas Story	Social Studies> Cultural anthropology: Amazing ancient cultures of the world Story	Science> Earth science: Clouds and weather Story	Literature> Human & animals: The friendship between a girl and a horse Story
Book 5	Social Studies> Ethics: Rules in daily life Story	Science>Biology: The five senses Report	Social Studies> Cultural anthropology: Astonishing festivals Report	Art>Music: Stories from two operas Story	Social Studies> World culture & history: The Renaissance Story	
Book 6	Social Studies> World geography & travel: Tourist attractions around the world Story	Science>Biology> Animal: Dinosaurs Story	Science> Astronomy: The solar system Story	Social Studies> People: Three great people who overcame hardships Story	Science>Scientific technology: The wonderful world of robots Report	
Book 7		Social Studies> Cultural anthropology: Mythological monsters from around the world Report		Science & Social Studies> Technology & culture: Inventions from around the world Report	Art>Works of art: Famous paintings Report	
Book 8				Social Studies> History: The California Gold Rush Report	Social Studies & Science> Psychology: Psychology in everyday life Story	
Book 9						
Book 10						

* 10 books in each level will be published.

How to Use This Book

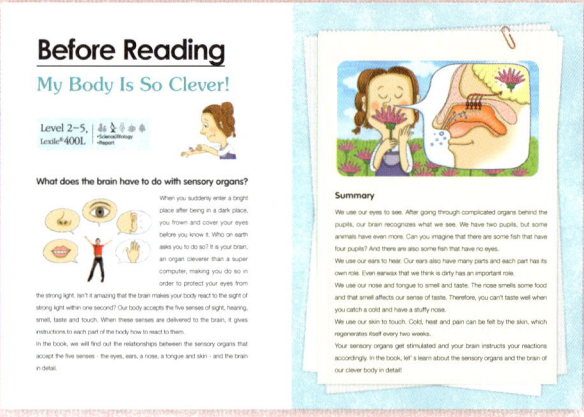

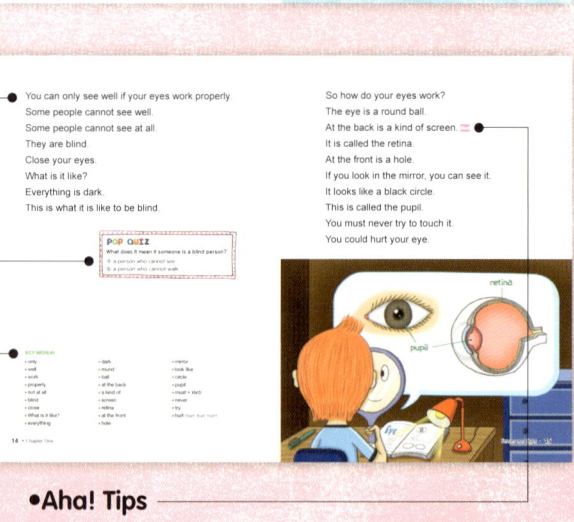

•Before Reading

You can easily find the topic and what kind of story you are about to read.

•The text

All the stories were written by professional writers from the U.S. and England, so you will read authentic and appropriate English sentences and expressions in every book in the series.

•Pop Quiz

Check out right away if you understand what you have just read by solving a pop quiz that checks your comprehension.

•Key Words

The key words and expressions on each page are listed for you to easily study them.

•Aha! Tips

Download free Korean explanations at *www.ihappyhouse.co.kr* for all of the sentences marked with "Aha!". These explain cultural, scientific, and economic knowledge or they deal with aspects of English such as grammatical structures or idiomatic expressions. There are lots of "Aha! Tips" to help you understand the text.

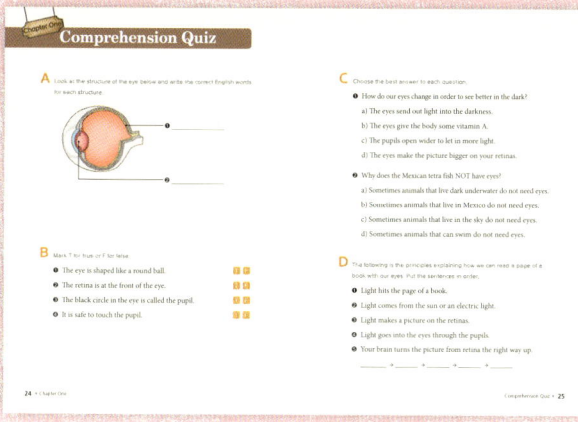

•Comprehension Quiz

After reading one chapter, solve various questions to find out if you fully understand the content.

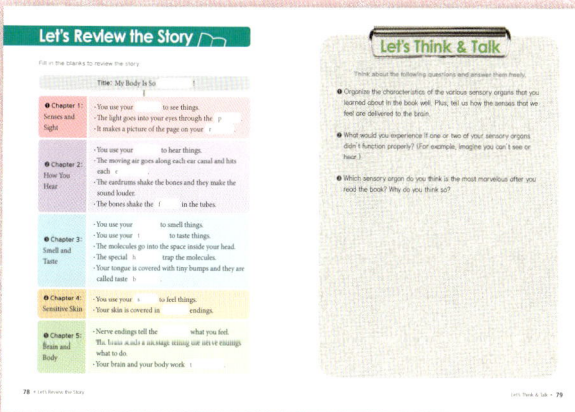

•Let's Review the Story /
•Let's Think & Talk

Fill in the blanks in the organizer to summarize the whole story. Express your own thinking and feelings about the story by answering the questions. You can build up logic and reasoning skills for your essay examinations in the future.

Appendix

Audio CD

In the CD audio book form, the texts are read vividly by American professional voice actors.

After-reading Test

Solve an additionally provided After-reading Test for each book.

The Korean translation, Answer Keys, a Word Quiz, a Word List, and Aha! Tips for each book

You can download them for free at *www.ihappyhouse.co.kr*

Before Reading

My Body Is So Clever!

| Level 2-5, Lexile® 400L | • Science)Biology • Report |

What does the brain have to do with sensory organs?

When you suddenly enter a bright place after being in a dark place, you frown and cover your eyes before you know it. Who on earth asks you to do so? It is your brain, an organ cleverer than a super computer, making you do so in order to protect your eyes from the strong light. Isn't it amazing that the brain makes your body react to the sight of strong light within one second? Our body accepts the five senses of sight, hearing, smell, taste and touch. When these senses are delivered to the brain, it gives instructions to each part of the body how to react to them.

In the book, we will find out the relationships between the sensory organs that accept the five senses - the eyes, ears, a nose, a tongue and skin - and the brain in detail.

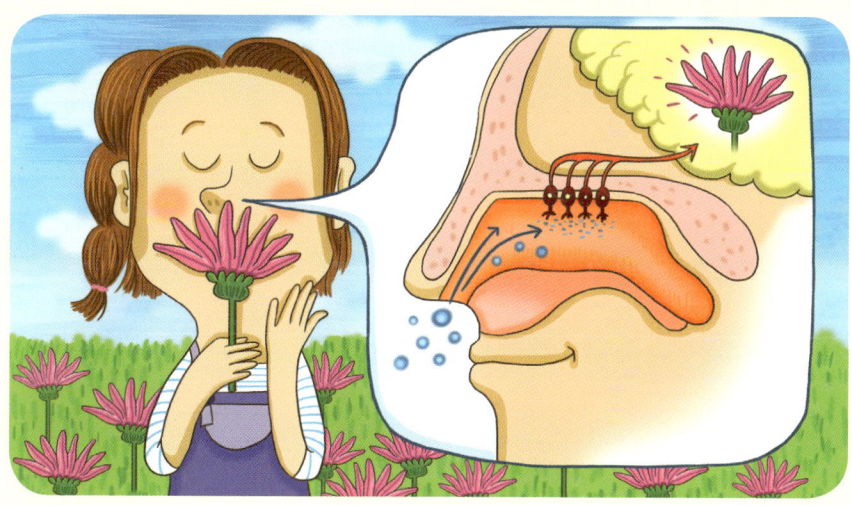

Summary

We use our eyes to see. After going through complicated organs behind the pupils, our brain recognizes what we see. We have two pupils, but some animals have even more. Can you imagine that there are some fish that have four pupils? And there are also some fish that have no eyes.

We use our ears to hear. Our ears also have many parts and each part has its own role. Even earwax that we think is dirty has an important role.

We use our nose and tongue to smell and taste. The nose smells some food and that smell affects our sense of taste. Therefore, you can't taste well when you catch a cold and have a stuffy nose.

We use our skin to touch. Cold, heat and pain can be felt by the skin, which regenerates itself every two weeks.

Your sensory organs get stimulated and your brain instructs your reactions accordingly. In the book, let's learn about the sensory organs and the brain of our clever body in detail!

Contents

My Body Is So Clever!

My Body Is So Clever!

Senses and Sight

You are holding this book in your hands. Aha!

You can feel it with your fingers.

You can see it with your eyes.

KEY WORDS

- sense
- sight
- hold (hold-held-held)
- can

- feel (feel-felt-felt)
- finger
- see (see-saw-seen)

Lift the book to your nose and take a sniff.
Can you smell it too?
Flick through the pages.
Can you hear the sound
that the pages make?
Can you feel air moving
against your skin?
You are using some of
your senses.

KEY WORDS

- lift
- take a sniff (take-took-taken)
- smell
- too
- flick through
- page
- hear (hear-heard-heard)

- sound
- air
- moving (cf. move)
- against
- skin
- use

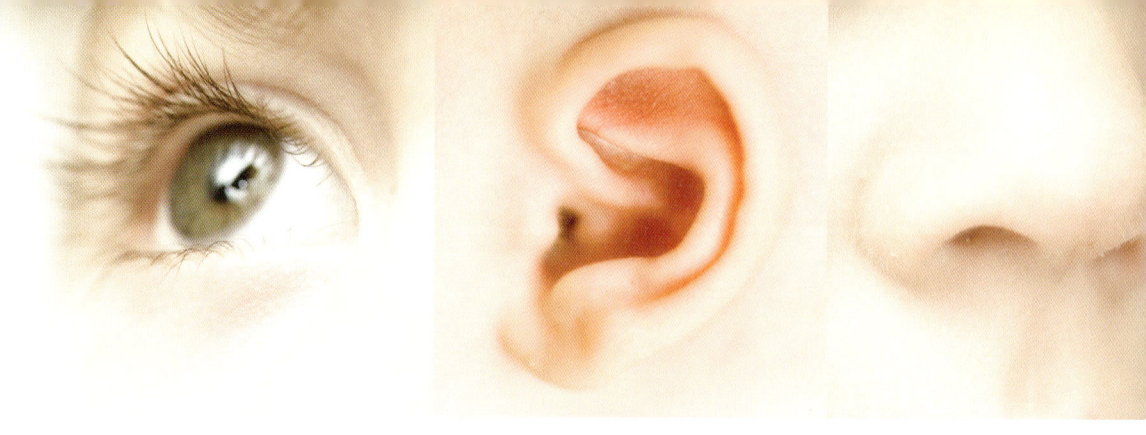

You have five senses.

They are: sight, hearing, smell, taste, and touch.

Your senses help you to live in the world.

They tell you what is around you.

KEY WORDS

- hearing
- taste
- touch
- help
- live
- world
- tell (tell-told-told)
- around
- mean (mean-meant-meant)

- thing
- if
- look around
- light
- darkness
- different
- shape
- color
- object

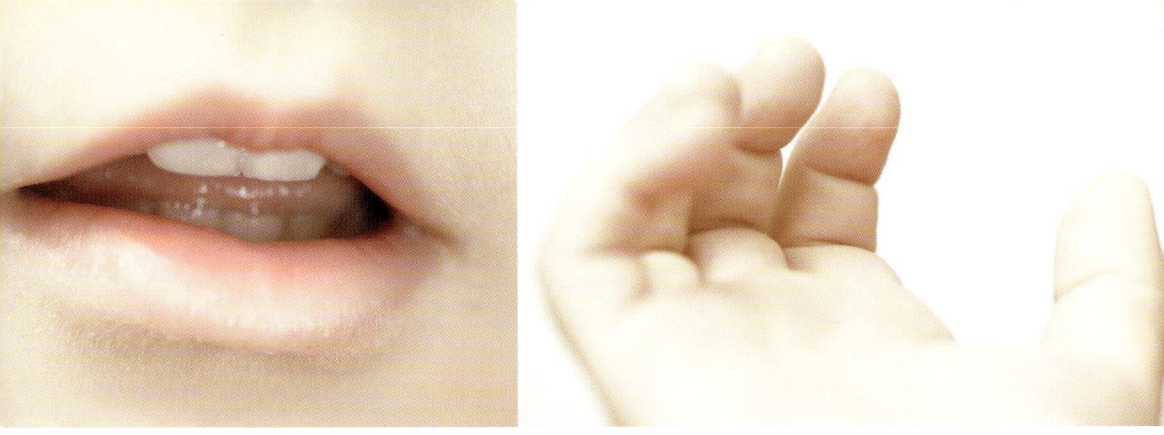

The sense of sight means that you can see things.

If you look around, you can see light and darkness.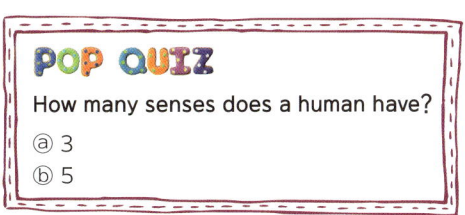

You can see different shapes.

You can see different colors.

You can see different objects.

POP QUIZ

How many senses does a human have?

ⓐ 3
ⓑ 5

You can only see well if your eyes work properly.

Some people cannot see well.

Some people cannot see at all.

They are blind.

Close your eyes.

What is it like?

Everything is dark.

This is what it is like to be blind.

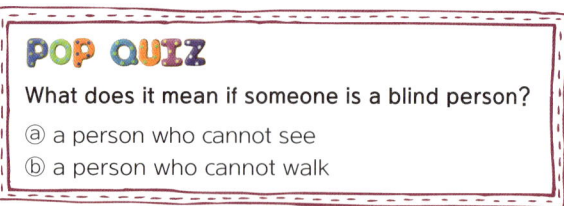

POP QUIZ

What does it mean if someone is a blind person?

ⓐ a person who cannot see
ⓑ a person who cannot walk

KEY WORDS

- only
- well
- work
- properly
- not at all
- blind
- close
- What is it like?
- everything

- dark
- round
- ball
- at the back
- a kind of
- screen
- retina
- at the front
- hole

- mirror
- look like
- circle
- pupil
- must + *Verb*
- never
- try
- hurt (hurt-hurt-hurt)

So how do your eyes work?

The eye is a round ball.

At the back is a kind of screen. Aha!

It is called the retina.

At the front is a hole.

If you look in the mirror, you can see it.

It looks like a black circle.

This is called the pupil.

You must never try to touch it.

You could hurt your eye.

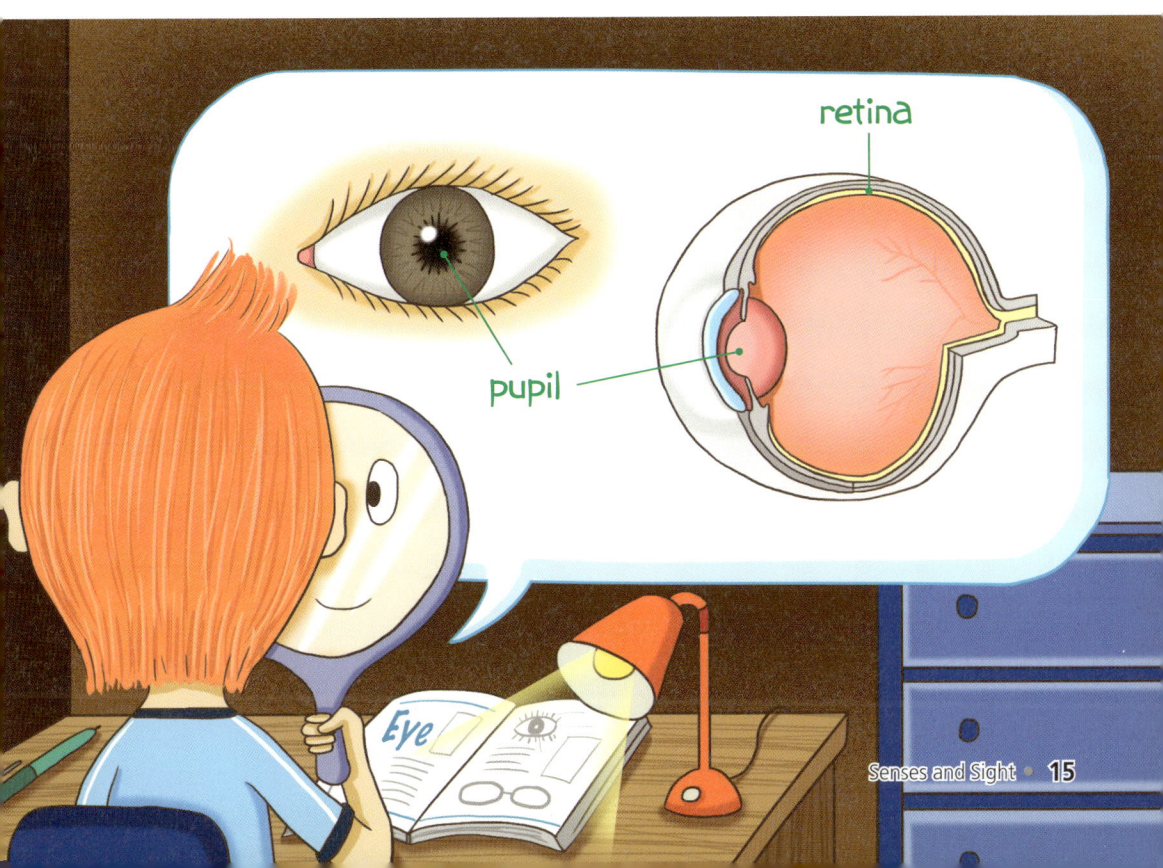

retina

pupil

Eye

Now, let's think about how you see this book.

Light comes from the sun, or from an electric light.

This light hits the page.

It bounces off the page and up to your eyes.

The light goes into your eyes through the pupils.

It makes a picture of the page on your retinas.

It is a bit like the picture on a TV screen.

But the picture is upside down!

Your brain is very clever.

It turns the picture the right way up.

Then, you can see the page.

This is how you see everything.

KEY WORDS

- **let's** (= let us)
- **think** (think-thought-thought)
- **about**
- **come from** (come-came-come)
- **electric light**
- **hit** (hit-hit-hit)
- **bounce off**
- **up to**
- **go into** (go-went-gone)
- **through**

- **a bit**
- **upside down**
- **brain**
- **clever**
- **turn**
- **right way up**
- **then**
- **together**
- **have to + Verb**

Your eyes and your brain work together.

You do not have to think about it.

Your body is so clever!

Can you see in the dark?

If there is a little light, you may see something.

Your pupils open wider to let in more light.

[in the light]　　　　　　　[in the dark]

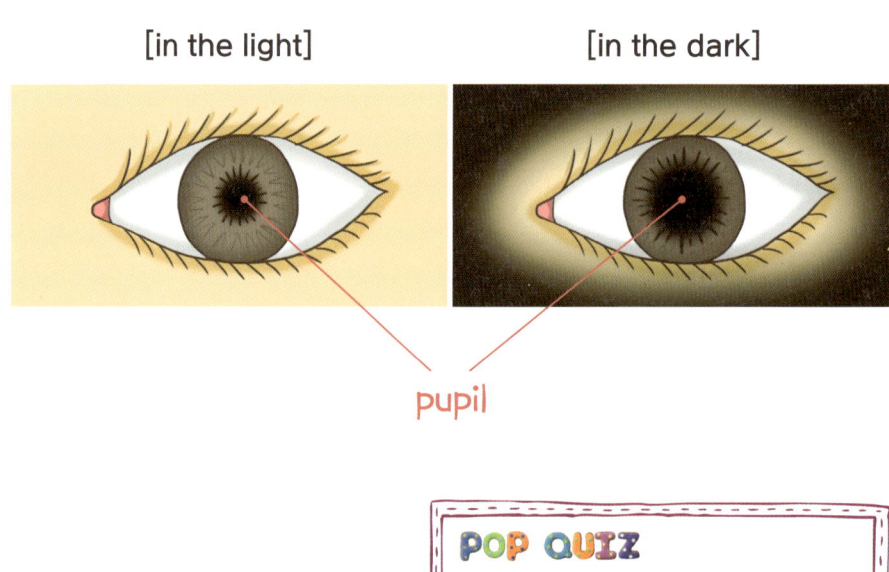

pupil

KEY WORDS

- a little
- may
- open (↔ close)
- wider
- let in (let-let-let)
- carrot
- be able to (= can)

- true
- contain
- vitamin A
- important
- healthy
- a few
- people (*cf.* person)

- enough
- find (find-found-found)
- difficult (↔ easy)
- already
- make no difference (make-made-made)

Many people think that if you eat carrots, you will be able to see in the dark.

Is this true?

Carrots contain vitamin A.

This vitamin is important for healthy eyes.

A few people don't get enough vitamin A.

They find it difficult to see at night.

But if you are already healthy, eating carrots makes no difference.

▲ foods that contain vitamin A

Many animals have excellent vision.

Predators are animals that catch and eat other animals.

Prey animals are eaten by others.

They both need good vision.

The predators need to find something to eat.

Hawks and eagles can see a tiny mouse from high in the sky.

They dive down and catch it.

▲ hawk

▲ eagle

KEY WORDS

- excellent
- vision
- predator
- catch (catch-caught-caught)
- other
- prey

- both
- need
- hawk
- eagle
- tiny
- dive down

▲ a giraffe which can see behind it

Prey animals often have eyes on the sides of their head.

This means that they can see behind them as well as in front.

Giraffes are a good example of this.

They can see predators approaching from behind.

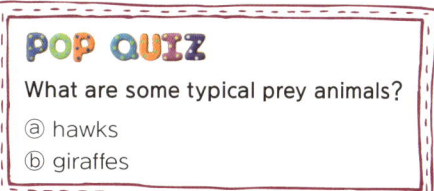

POP QUIZ

What are some typical prey animals?

ⓐ hawks

ⓑ giraffes

KEY WORDS

- often
- on the sides of the head
- behind
- A as well as B

- front
- giraffe
- an example of
- approach

There are some fish in South America called "four-eyed fish."

They only have two eyes.

But each eye is divided in half.

Each half of the eye has its own pupil.

This means that the fish can see above and below water at the same time.

▲ four-eyed fish

KEY WORDS

- fish
- South America
- four-eyed fish
- each
- be divided
- in half
- own
- above
- below
- at the same time
- tarsier
- rainforest

- creature
- nocturnal
- awake
- large
- grapefruit
- cave
- poor
- completely
- all the time
- Mexican tetra
- deep
- under the water

▲ tarsier

The tarsier is a rainforest creature.

It is nocturnal.

This means that it is awake at night.

It has very large eyes so it can see well in the dark.

If you were a tarsier, your eyes would be as big as grapefruits! Aha!

Animals that live in caves have poor vision.

In some caves, it is completely dark all the time.

The Mexican tetra fish live in deep caves under the water.

They have no eyes at all! There is no light, so they do not need eyes.

▲ Mexican tetra

Comprehension Quiz

A Look at the structure of the eye below and write the correct English words for each structure.

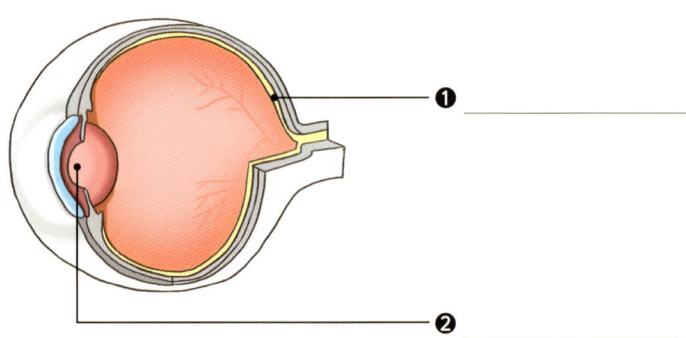

❶ _____

❷ _____

B Mark T for true or F for false.

❶ The eye is shaped like a round ball.　　　　　　　T　F

❷ The retina is at the front of the eye.　　　　　　　T　F

❸ The black circle in the eye is called the pupil.　　T　F

❹ It is safe to touch the pupil.　　　　　　　　　　T　F

C Choose the best answer to each question.

❶ How do our eyes change in order to see better in the dark?

a) The eyes send out light into the darkness.

b) The eyes give the body some vitamin A.

c) The pupils open wider to let in more light.

d) The eyes make the picture bigger on your retinas.

❷ Why does the Mexican tetra fish NOT have eyes?

a) Sometimes animals that live dark underwater do not need eyes.

b) Sometimes animals that live in Mexico do not need eyes.

c) Sometimes animals that live in the sky do not need eyes.

d) Sometimes animals that can swim do not need eyes.

D The following is the principles explaining how we can read a page of a book with our eyes. Put the sentences in order.

❶ Light hits the page of a book.

❷ Light comes from the sun or an electric light.

❸ Light makes a picture on the retinas.

❹ Light goes into the eyes through the pupils.

❺ Your brain turns the picture from retina the right way up.

_____ → _____ → _____ → _____ → _____

How You Hear

Now, let's think about how you hear sounds. Aha!

Put your hands over your ears.

Can you still hear clearly?

People who cannot hear are deaf.

Find a mirror.

Look at the reflection of your face.

You can see part of each ear.

KEY WORDS

- **put** (put-put-put)
- over
- still
- clearly

- deaf
- reflection
- part

There is a part of each ear on the outside of your head.

This part is shaped to collect sounds.

Some animals have big ears.

They are shaped to collect sound waves.

This means that they can hear quiet sounds more easily.

POP QUIZ

Mark T for true or F for false.

If some animals have big ears, they can hear quiet sounds more easily. T / F

KEY WORDS

- outside (↔ inside)
- collect
- sound wave

- quiet (↔ loud)
- easily

Ask a friend to stand beside you.

Tell him or her to whisper something quietly.

Now put your hand behind your ear.

Curl it into a round shape.

Tell your friend to whisper again.

Can you hear the whisper better?

KEY WORDS

- ask
- **stand** (stand-stood-stood)
- beside

- whisper
- quietly
- curl

- again
- better

Rabbits have ears that are shaped to collect sound.

They can also turn their ears from side to side.

This helps them to find out where the sound is coming from.

They need to hear very well indeed.

Lots of predators want to catch them.

Rabbits need good hearing to know when a predator is coming.

Then, they can run away.

POP QUIZ

Why do rabbits need to listen to sounds so well?

ⓐ Rabbits need to catch their prey easily.

ⓑ Rabbits need to run away from lots of predators.

KEY WORDS

- also
- from side to side
- find out

- indeed
- lots of
- know (know-knew-known)

- run away (run-ran-run)

Bats have excellent hearing.

They fly at night, when it is difficult to see.

They make tiny clicking sounds.

Humans cannot hear them, but a bat can.

The sounds bounce off buildings and trees.

They also bounce off insects.

By listening carefully, the bat knows what is around it.

It knows where the insects are.

This makes it easy to catch them.

KEY WORDS

- bat
- **fly** (fly-flew-flown)
- clicking
- human
- listen
- carefully
- most of
- in the side of

- ear canal
- be full of
- hair
- sticky
- wax
- **keep** (keep-kept-kept)
- clean
- stop

Most of your ear is inside your head.

There are holes in the side of your head.

If you look in the mirror, you can see them.

Each one is called an ear canal.

They are full of tiny hairs and sticky wax.

They help to keep it clean.

They stop things getting inside your ear.

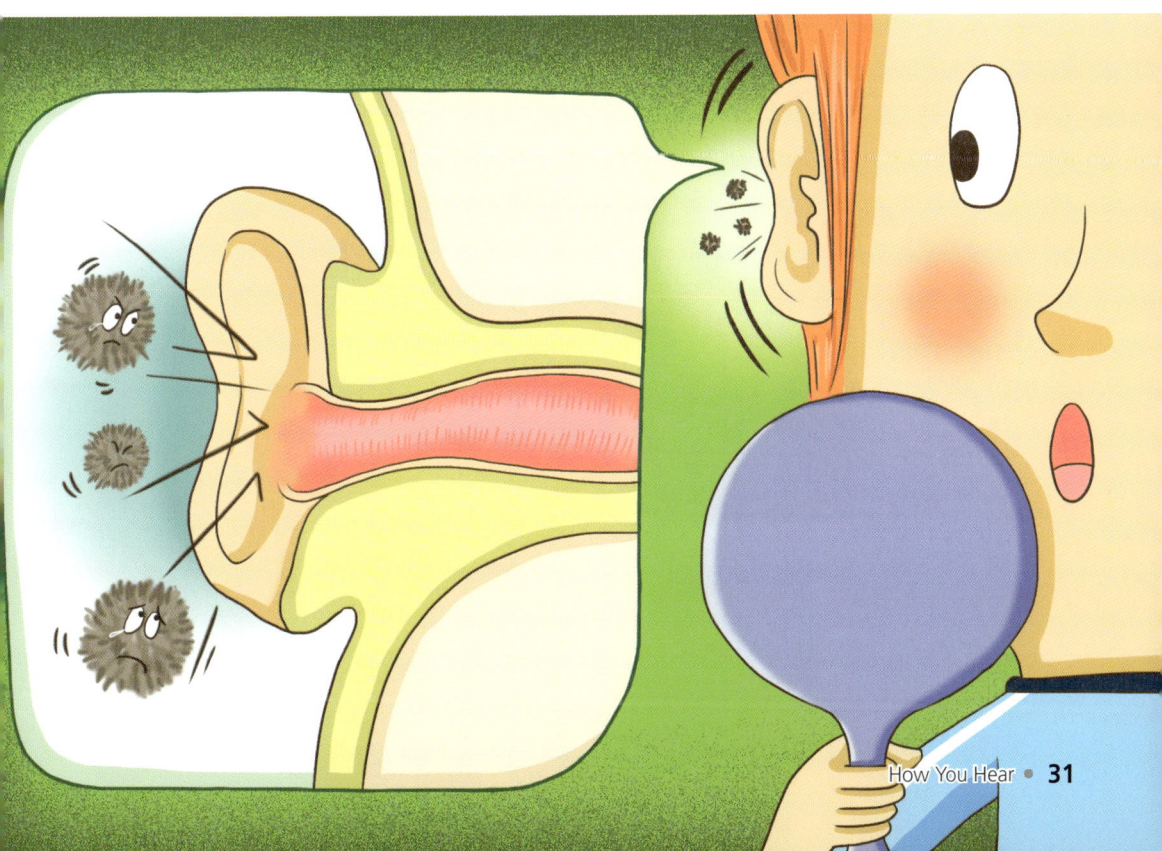

At the end of the ear canal, there is a thin piece of skin.

It is stretched tight, like a drum.

It is called the eardrum.

Yes, there is a drum inside your head!

On the other side of the eardrum, there are three tiny bones.

They are the smallest bones in your body.

They are about 3mm long.

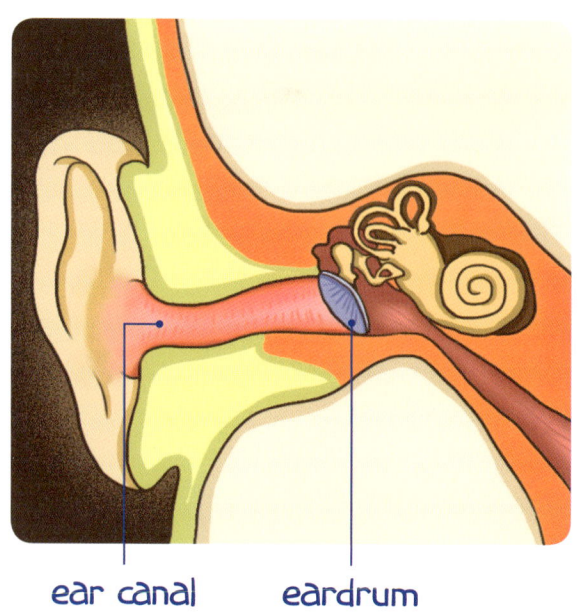

ear canal   eardrum

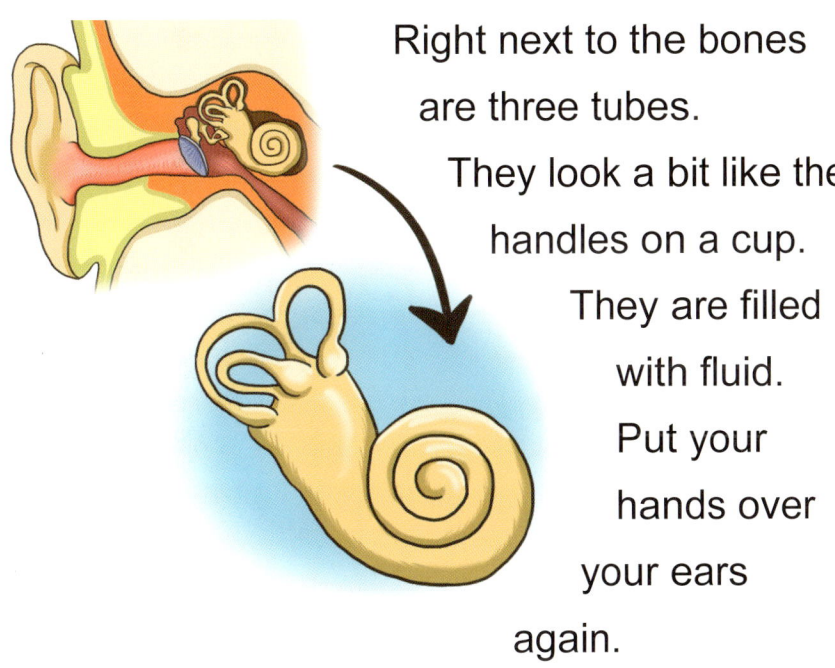

Right next to the bones
are three tubes.
They look a bit like the
handles on a cup.
They are filled
with fluid.
Put your
hands over
your ears
again.
Can you hear a sound like a rushing river?
That is the fluid moving about inside your ears.

KEY WORDS

- thin
- piece
- stretch
- tight
- drum
- eardrum
- the other side
- bone

- smallest
- right next to
- tube
- handle
- be filled with
- fluid
- rushing (*cf.* rush)

So how do your ears work?

How can you hear a sound?

A sound is made when something vibrates.

This means that it moves very quickly.

Often, the movement is too fast to see. Aha!

The movement also makes the air vibrate.

You can see how this works in a bathtub.

Get into a bathtub full of water.

Tap the side of the bathtub.

▲ waves in the water

You will see tiny waves in the water.

The same thing happens in air, but you cannot see the waves.

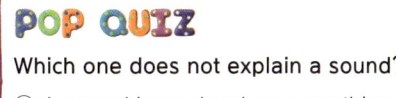

POP QUIZ

Which one does not explain a sound?

ⓐ A sound is made when something vibrates.
ⓑ You can see the sound waves in the air.

KEY WORDS

- bathtub
- get into (get-got-gotten)
- tap
- wave
- same
- happen

The moving air goes into your ears.

It goes along each ear canal.

It hits each eardrum, which vibrates too.

The eardrums shake the bones.

The bones make the sound louder.

The bones shake the fluid in the tubes.

KEY WORDS

- along
- shake (shake-shook-shaken)
- louder

Your brain senses the fluid moving.

From this, your brain knows what the sound was.

This is how you hear a sound.

Your ears and your brain work together.

You do not have to think about it.

Your body is so clever!

Comprehension Quiz

A Choose the hearing organ in the picture that belongs to the explanation below.

> • It is at the end of the ear canal.
>
> • It is a thin piece of skin.
>
> • It is stretched tight, like a drum.

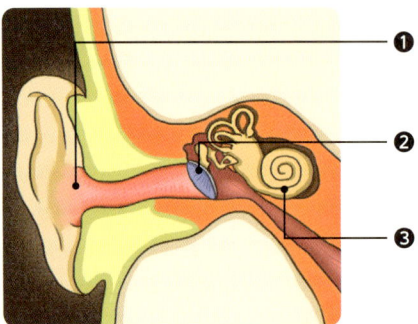

B Rearrange the following sentences according to the processes in which we hear a sound.

❶ Your brain senses the fluid moving and knows what the sound is.

❷ The three tiny bones shake the fluid in the tubes.

❸ Moving air goes into the ear canal and hits the eardrum.

❹ The eardrum shakes the three tiny bones.

_____ → _____ → _____ → _____

C Fill in each blank with the right word below.

| collect | handles | fluid | clicking |

❶ Bats make tiny _____ sounds.

❷ Rabbits have big ears that are shaped to _____ sound.

❸ The three tubes are full of _____ which moves about.

❹ The three tubes are shaped like the _____ of a cup.

D Solve the crossword puzzle.

Across

❸ Which sense do your ears help with?

❹ What do we call people who cannot hear?

Down

❶ There are _____ tiny bones in each ear.

❷ The sticky _____ helps to keep an ear canal clean.

Smell and Taste

Now, let's think about how you smell something.

You smell with your nose.

Breathe in through your nose.

What can you smell now?

KEY WORDS

- breathe in
- size
- nostril

- open into
- space

Noses are different shapes and sizes.

Some are big.

Some are small.

Some are long.

Some are short.

All noses have holes in them.

Human noses have two holes.

These holes are called nostrils.

They open into a space inside your head.

So how do you smell something?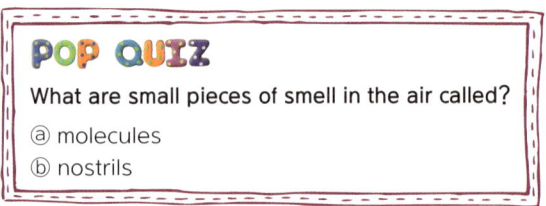

Breathe in through your nose.

Can you feel air coming in?

It comes in through your nostrils.

In the air are tiny pieces of the smell.

They are too small to see.

They are called molecules.

The smell of a flower is one kind of molecule.

The smell of cooking meat is another.

The smell of this book is another.

POP QUIZ

What are small pieces of smell in the air called?

ⓐ molecules
ⓑ nostrils

KEY WORDS

- molecule
- cook
- meat
- another
- float into
- float about

- special
- stick out (stick-stuck-stuck)
- trap
- send (send-sent-sent)
- message

The molecules float into your nostrils.

They go into the space inside your head.

The molecules float about inside the space.

There are some special hairs.

They stick out into the space.

They trap the smell molecules.

They send a message to your brain.

Your brain tells you what the smell is.

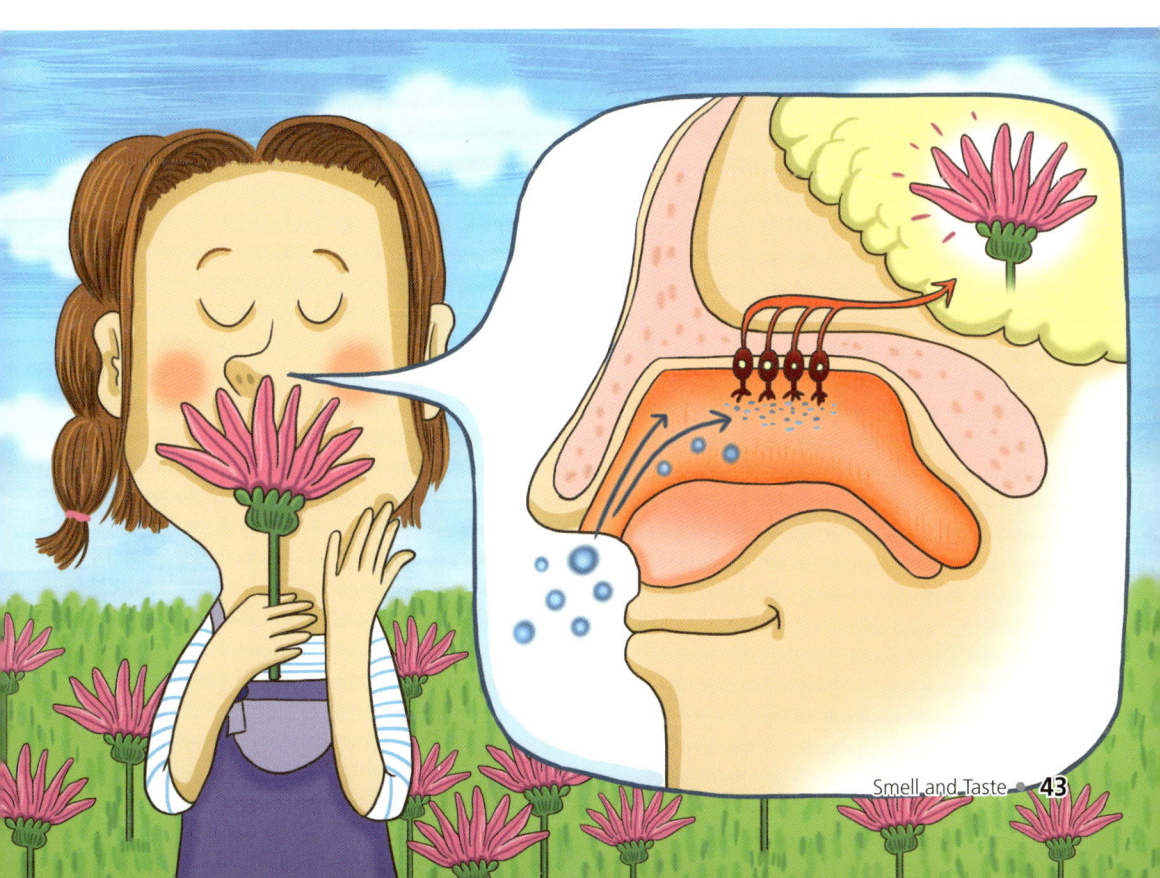

This is how you smell everything. Your nose and your brain work together. You do not have to think about it. Your body is so clever!

POP QUIZ

Mark T for true or F for false.

Your nose and your brain don't work together.

T / F

KEY WORDS

- job
- perfume
- maker
- mix
- right
- pleasant
- safety inspector
- chemical

- smoke
- detect
- disease
- diabetes
- breath
- certain
- nail polish remover

Some jobs need a good sense of smell.
Perfume makers mix the right smells to make
pleasant perfumes. **Aha!**
Safety inspectors smell chemicals or smoke in
the air.
Doctors can detect some diseases by their smell.
Some people have a disease called diabetes.
Their breath may have a certain smell.
It smells like nail polish remover.

Now, let's think about how you taste something.

What is your favorite taste?

Perhaps it is something sweet, like cookies.

Perhaps it is something salty, like potato chips.

Perhaps it is something sour, like a lemon.

Perhaps it is something bitter, like unsweetened tea.

You taste things with your tongue.

Look in a mirror.

Stick out your tongue.

What does it look like?

It is covered with tiny bumps.

These are called taste buds.

Taste buds can sense four kinds of taste.

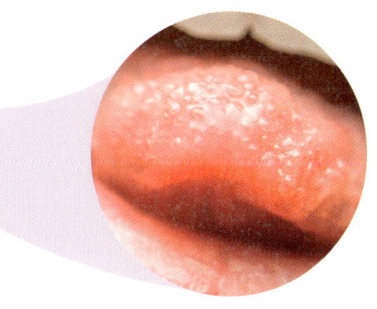

KEY WORDS

- tongue
- be covered with

- bump
- taste bud

Smell and Taste • **47**

There are taste buds all over your tongue.

They can taste sweet, salty, sour and bitter tastes.

They can tell the difference between these tastes.

Every flavor is made up of these four tastes combined together.

Everything that you eat or drink has a flavor.

The flavor can be mostly one of these four tastes.

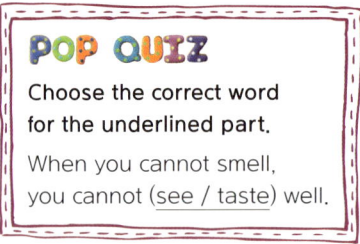

POP QUIZ

Choose the correct word for the underlined part.

When you cannot smell, you cannot (see / taste) well.

KEY WORDS

- all over
- tell the difference
- between
- every
- flavor

- be made up of
- combine
- drink (drink-drank-drunk)
- mostly

Some flavors are mostly sweet.

Some flavors are mostly sour.

Or the flavor can be a mixture of the four tastes.

But the tongue cannot taste things on its own.

The nose and the tongue work together.

When you cannot smell, you cannot taste.

So when you have a stuffy nose, food has no taste. Aha!

KEY WORDS

- mixture
- on one's own
- stuffy
- have no taste

Smell and Taste • **49**

How does this happen?

When you eat something, molecules go into your mouth.

The molecules go straight into the nose, too.

Your mouth and your nose are joined at the back.

So some molecules go up into your nose from the mouth.

Your brain puts together the smell and the four tastes.

It knows the flavor of the food or drink.

This is how you taste everything.

Your tongue, your nose and your brain work together.

You do not have to think about it.

Your body is so clever!

KEY WORDS

- go straight into
- join

- go up into
- put together

50 • Chapter Three

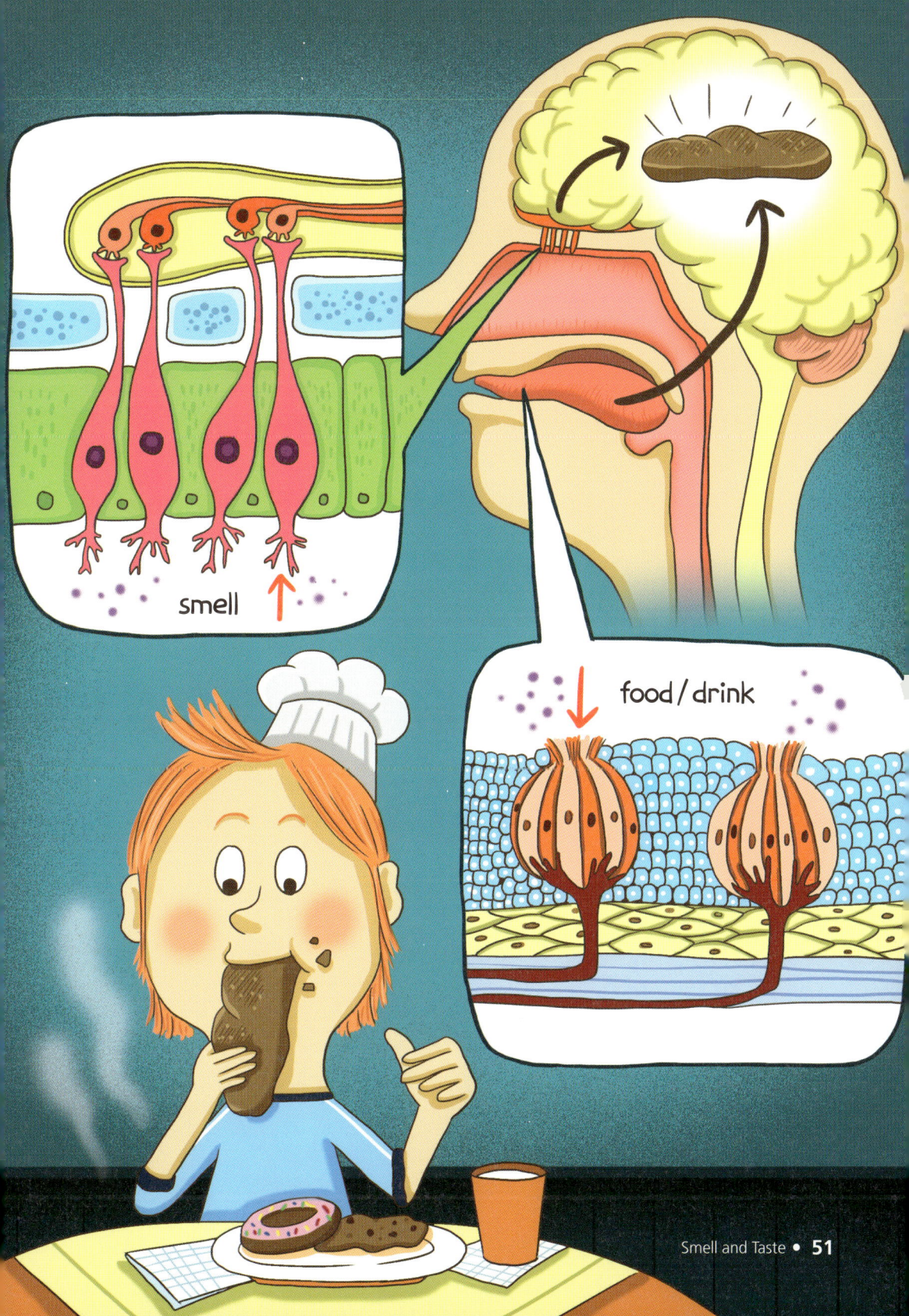

smell

food / drink

Comprehension Quiz

A Mark T for true or F for false.

❶ The tiny bumps on your tongue are called taste buds. T F

❷ The tongue can taste things on its own. T F

❸ The nose helps the tongue to taste. T F

❹ Your mouth and your nose are joined at the back. T F

B Fill in each blank with the right word below.

hairs	nostrils	nose	molecules

❶ Humans have two holes in their _____.

❷ The air comes in through your _____.

❸ Tiny pieces called _____ go into a space inside the head.

❹ There are special _____ to trap the molecules in the space inside the head.

C

Choose the best answer to each question.

❶ Who is NOT mentioned as a person who needs an excellent sense of smell?

a) a perfume maker

b) a doctor

c) a dressmaker

d) a safety inspector

❷ Which of the following explanation is wrong?

a) There are taste buds all over your tongue.

b) Tiny pieces of the smell are too small to see.

c) Taste buds can sense only one kind of taste.

d) When your nose is stuffy, food has no taste.

D

Rearrange the statements in the correct order to explain how we can smell.

❶ Your brain tells you what the smell is.

❷ You breathe air into your nostrils.

❸ The hairs send a message to your brain.

❹ The molecules are trapped by hairs in the space inside your head.

❺ The molecules go into the space inside your head.

_____ → _____ → _____ → _____ → _____

Sensitive Skin

The fifth sense is the sense of touch. **Aha!**

For this, your skin and your brain work together.

Your skin covers your body.

On the bottom of your feet, it is thick.

This protects you when you walk.

In other places, your skin is thinner.

Your skin sends you messages all the time.

It is amazing!

The skin can feel different things.

It can feel heat and cold.

It can feel hard things and soft things.

It can feel pain.

Now, let's think about how you feel something.

Your skin is covered in nerve endings.

These are special cells.

They send messages to your brain.

They have different jobs.

KEY WORDS

- sensitive
- fifth
- cover
- on the bottom of
- feet
- thick (↔ thin)
- protect
- place
- thinner

- amazing
- heat
- cold
- hard
- soft
- pain
- nerve ending
- cell

Some nerve endings feel heat and cold.

Most nerve endings feel pain.

Other nerve endings feel things that press on them.

They tell your brain what is going on.

Imagine that you have an itch.

Nerve endings send a message to your brain.

"Something is itching!" the message says.

pain

heat

cold

press

The brain sends a message to your fingers.

It tells them to scratch the skin.

Then the itch may go away.

Some parts of your skin are more sensitive than others.

This means that they feel things more strongly.

They have more nerve endings.

Your lips are very sensitive.

Your fingertips are very sensitive, too.

It is important that we can feel things.

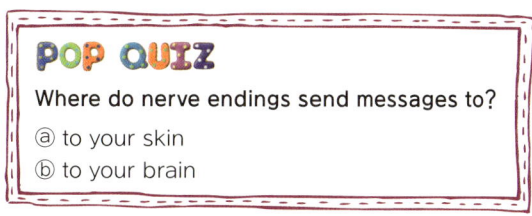

POP QUIZ

Where do nerve endings send messages to?

ⓐ to your skin
ⓑ to your brain

The nerve endings in our skin keep us safe.

What happens if you touch something hot?

The nerve endings send a message to the brain.

"Something is too hot!" the message says.

The brain sends a message to your hand.

It tells your hand to move.

It moves away from the hot thing.

This is how you feel everything.

Your skin and your brain work together.

You do not have to think about it.

Your body is so clever!

Look closely at your skin.

The skin that you see is not the same skin that you had a month ago!

Your skin cells die all the time.

They fall off without you noticing.

Do you have dust under your bed?

Some of that dust is made of your dead skin cells!

Luckily, your skin makes new cells all the time.

Every two to four weeks, your skin replaces itself completely.

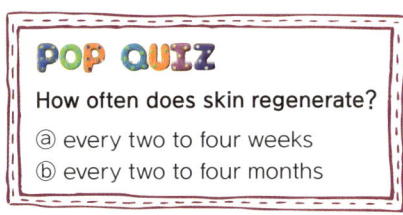

POP QUIZ

How often does skin regenerate?

ⓐ every two to four weeks
ⓑ every two to four months

KEY WORDS

- keep ~ safe
- move away from
- closely
- month
- ago
- die
- fall off (fall-fell-fallen)
- without
- notice
- dust
- be made of
- dead
- luckily
- replace
- itself

Some people have skin that is too sensitive.

It is red and itchy.

It gets sore very easily. Aha!

Other people have very dry skin.

They have to be careful what soap they use.

They have to rub in special cream every day.

This keeps their skin smooth.

There are other skin problems, too.

People with these problems can feel very uncomfortable.

They may also feel embarrassed.

If you see some people with sore, red skin, don't stare at it.

Don't tease them about it.

Be kind and understanding.

Comprehension Quiz

A Fill in each blank with the right word(s) below.

| smooth   sensitive   die   nerve endings |

❶ Your skin is covered in _____ .

❷ Some parts of your skin are more _____ than others.

❸ Your skin cells _____ all the time.

❹ Some people have to rub in special cream every day to keep

their skin _____ .

B Mark T for true or F for false.

❶ You have different skin today than you had two
months ago.   T F

❷ The nerve endings in our skin keep us safe.   T F

❸ Your skin on the bottom of your feet is thin.   T F

❹ Sensitive parts of your skin have more nerve endings.   T F

C Choose the best answer to each question.

❶ What do nerve endings do?

a) They keep your skin soft.

b) They send messages to your brain.

c) They help you to walk.

d) They make you go to sleep.

❷ What happens when skin cells die?

a) Dead cells feel pain.

b) Dead cells make the skin soft.

c) Dead cells fall off without you noticing.

d) Dead cells go to your brain.

D Rearrange the following sentences according to the order that skin sensations are delivered to the brain.

❶ The nerve endings send a message to your brain.

❷ Your fingers scratch the itch.

❸ Something itches your skin.

❹ Your brain tells your fingers to move.

_____ → _____ → _____ → _____

Brain and Body

Your senses work with your brain.

Your brain connects with the nerves all over your body.

Nerve endings tell the brain what they feel.

They send messages to the brain.

The brain receives the messages.

It sends back information about what to do.

If a sound is too loud, it might damage your ears.

So your brain tells your hands to cover your ears.

KEY WORDS

- connect
- receive
- send back
- information
- damage
- What if ~?
- bright

- shine
- first
- less
- reach
- probably
- a little bit
- block out

What if a bright light shines into your eyes?

First, your brain makes the pupils smaller.

Then, less light reaches the retinas.

After that your brain probably tells you to close your eyes a little bit.

Or it might tell you to put your hand in front of your face.

All these things block out the light.

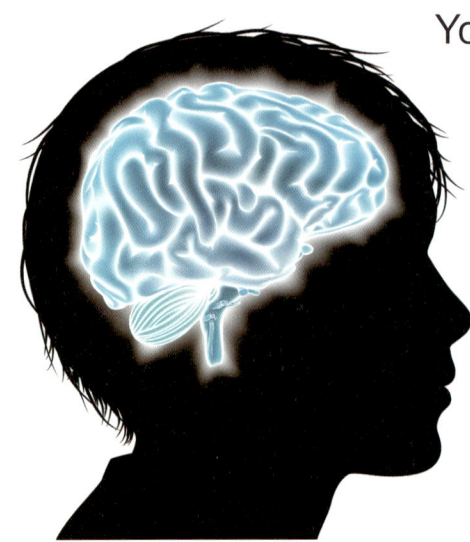

Your brain is more powerful than any computer. Aha!
It receives millions of messages every minute.
It controls your breathing.
It controls your heart rate.
It helps you to digest food.
It stores memories from your whole life.
It thinks billions of thoughts.
Even when you are asleep, it works hard.

KEY WORDS

- powerful
- millions of
- minute
- control
- breathing
- heart rate
- digest

- store
- memory
- whole life (cf. life)
- billions of
- thought
- even
- asleep

Make your hands into fists.

Now put them together, side by side.

This is about the size of your brain.

It is a grayish color.

The brain is quite soft.

This means that it must be protected.

So it is hidden inside the hard, bony skull.

This helps to prevent damage to it.

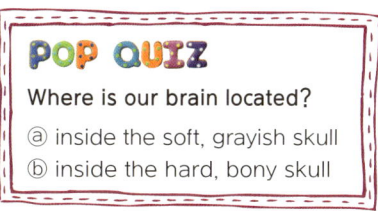

POP QUIZ

Where is our brain located?

ⓐ inside the soft, grayish skull

ⓑ inside the hard, bony skull

KEY WORDS

- fist
- side by side
- grayish
- quite

- hide (hide-hid-hidden)
- bony
- skull
- prevent

Different parts of the brain control different things.

Some parts help you to speak.

Others help you to remember.

Different parts feel different emotions.

The left side is better at problem solving and math.

The right side is creative.

It helps you to draw or tell stories.

KEY WORDS

- **speak** (speak-spoke-spoken)
- **remember**
- **emotion**
- **problem solving**

- **math**
- **creative**
- **draw** (draw-drew-drawn)
- **story**

68 • Chapter Five

Your brain works best when you get enough sleep. Have you ever been in school when you are tired?  It's difficult to think properly! It is important that you eat healthy foods.

Many experts say that fish is very good for your brain.

You should drink plenty of water, too.

These things help your brain to work at its best.

They help your senses to work properly, too.

KEY WORDS

- best
- get enough sleep
- Have you ever + p.p.?
- tired
- expert

- be good for
- should + *Verb*
- plenty of
- at one's best

Brain and Body • **69**

Some people cannot use all of their senses.

Sometimes this happens because of a disease. Aha!

Sometimes it happens because their brain is damaged.

Sometimes they are born that way.

Life is harder for them.

But they can use other senses instead.

Blind people cannot see.

But they can use their fingertips to read.

There is a special language called Braille.

The letters of the alphabet are turned into patterns of bumps.

Blind people can "read" the bumps with their fingers.

KEY WORDS

- sometimes
- be born
- that way
- harder
- instead
- language

- Braille
- letter
- alphabet
- be turned into
- pattern

BRAILLE Alphabet

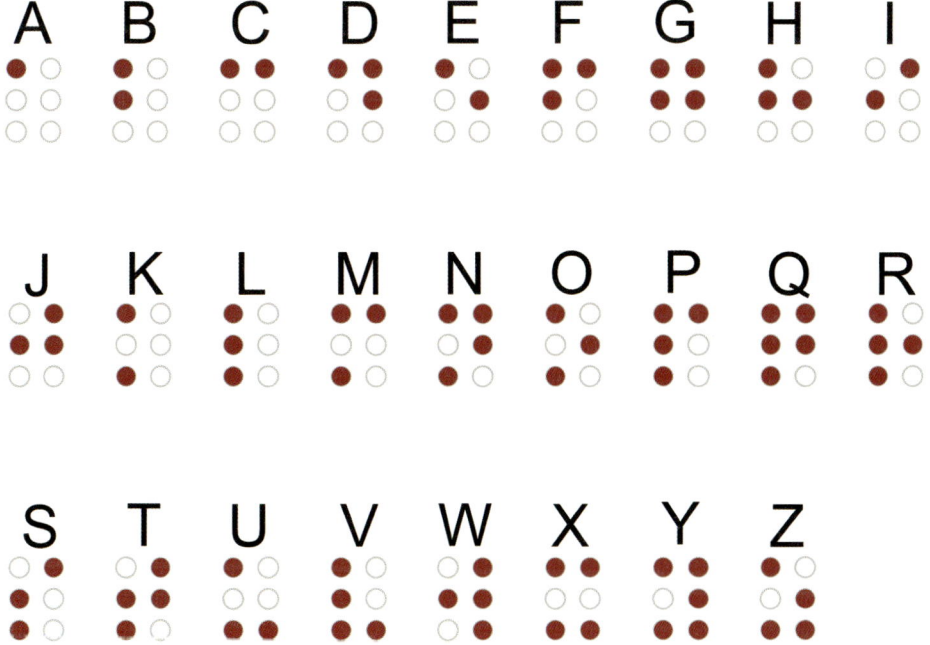

A B C D E F G H I

J K L M N O P Q R

S T U V W X Y Z

Deaf people cannot hear.

But they still understand what people say.

They use a special language.

It is called sign language.

Words are turned into hand movements.

Deaf people look at the hand movements.

They understand the words.

They also watch people's lips.

They can "read" people's lips.

They understand what the people are saying.

Some people cannot smell.

Sometimes an operation has made them lose their sense of smell.

Sometimes an accident has made them lose their sense of smell.

Sometimes they were born without a sense of smell.

This means that they cannot taste either.

Foods have no taste.

It is not very nice.

But they can still live a normal life.

KEY WORDS

- **understand** (understand-understood-understood)
- **sign language**
- **word**
- **watch**
- **operation**
- **lose** (lose-lost-lost)
- **accident**
- **either**
- **normal**

Some people cannot feel things on their skin.

This is because they have a disease.

Their nerve endings do not work properly.

This can be dangerous.

They do not know if they are touching something hot.

They do not know if something is hurting them.

So they must be very careful in everyday life.

POP QUIZ

Choose the right word(s) for the blank.

Some people cannot feel things on their skin because their _____ do not work properly.
ⓐ retinas
ⓑ nerve endings

KEY WORDS

- dangerous
- everyday life
- give (give-gave-given)
- danger

- bring (bring-brought-brought)
- pleasure
- make sure (that)
- take care of

Your senses and your brain work together.

They give you information about the world.

They protect you from danger.

They bring you pleasure.

Your body is so clever.

Make sure that you take care of it! Aha!

Comprehension Quiz

A Where does the brain function shown below work better, the left brain or the right brain? Circle between them.

❶ drawing   **the left brain / the right brain**

❷ problem solving   **the left brain / the right brain**

❸ telling stories   **the left brain / the right brain**

❹ math   **the left brain / the right brain**

B Mark T for true or F for false.

❶ Deaf people can understand what people are saying by "reading" their lips.   T F

❷ You should drink plenty of water to keep your brain best.   T F

❸ You should sleep less in order to make your brain work better.   T F

❹ Experts say that eating fish is bad for your brain.   T F

C Choose the best answer to each question.

❶ Which characteristic is NOT right about the brain?

a) Two fists are about the size of your brain.

b) It is a grayish color.

c) It is quite hard.

d) It is hidden inside the hard, bony skull.

❷ What will happen if you shine a bright light into your eyes?

a) Your pupils get smaller.

b) Your pupils get bigger.

c) Your retinas change color.

d) Your retinas get smaller.

D Fill in each blank with the right word below.

memories	asleep	digest	controls

❶ Your brain _____ your breathing.

❷ Your brain helps you to _____ food.

❸ Your brain stores _____ from your whole life.

❹ Even when you are _____, your brain works hard.

Let's Review the Story

Fill in the blanks to review the story.

Title: My Body Is So _____!

❶ Chapter 1: Senses and Sight	• You use your _____ to see things. • The light goes into your eyes through the p_____. • It makes a picture of the page on your r_____.
❷ Chapter 2: How You Hear	• You use your _____ to hear things. • The moving air goes along each ear canal and hits each e_____. • The eardrums shake the bones and they make the sound louder. • The bones shake the f_____ in the tubes.
❸ Chapter 3: Smell and Taste	• You use your _____ to smell things. • You use your t_____ to taste things. • The molecules go into the space inside your head. • The special h_____ trap the molecules. • Your tongue is covered with tiny bumps and they are called taste b_____.
❹ Chapter 4: Sensitive Skin	• You use your s_____ to feel things. • Your skin is covered in _____ endings.
❺ Chapter 5: Brain and Body	• Nerve endings tell the _____ what you feel. • The brain sends a message telling the nerve endings what to do. • Your brain and your body work t_____.

Let's Think & Talk

Think about the following questions and answer them freely.

❶ Organize the characteristics of the various sensory organs that you learned about in the book well. Plus, tell us how the senses that we feel are delivered to the brain.

❷ What would you experience if one or two of your sensory organs didn't function properly? (For example, imagine you can't see or hear.)

❸ Which sensory organ do you think is the most marvelous after you read the book? Why do you think so?

Let's Review the Story

Title: My Body Is So [Clever] !

❶ **Chapter 1:** Senses and Sight	• You use your [eyes] to see things. • The light goes into your eyes through the [pupils]. • It makes a picture of the page on your [retinas].
❷ **Chapter 2:** How You Hear	• You use your [ears] to hear things. • The moving air goes along each ear canal and hits each [eardrum]. • The eardrums shake the bones and they make the sound louder. • The bones shake the [fluid] in the tubes.
❸ **Chapter 3:** Smell and Taste	• You use your [nose] to smell things. • You use your [tongue] to taste things. • The molecules go into the space inside your head. • The special [hairs] trap the molecules. • Your tongue is covered with tiny bumps and they are called taste [buds].
❹ **Chapter 4:** Sensitive Skin	• You use your [skin] to feel things. • Your skin is covered in [nerve] endings.
❺ **Chapter 5:** Brain and Body	• Nerve endings tell the [brain] what you feel. • The brain sends a message telling the nerve endings what to do. • Your brain and your body work [together].

Smart Readers: **Wise** & **Wide**

After-reading Test

- My Body Is So Clever!
- Level 2
- 18 Questions

  (Vocabulary 5 / Reading Comprehension 10 /

  Sentence Structure & Grammar 3)

My Body Is So Clever! After-reading Test

1. Which pair has the wrong past tense form of the listed verb?
   ① hurt – hurt
   ② hit – hitted
   ③ know – knew
   ④ send – sent

2. Which of the following explains "a nocturnal animal" best?
   ① an animal that can see a long way
   ② an animal that lives in trees
   ③ an animal that eats other animals
   ④ an animal that is awake at night

3. Which one is the closest to the meaning of "vibrate" in the following sentence?

   Sound is made when something vibrates.

   ① stays still
   ② shakes quickly
   ③ gets wet
   ④ falls over

4. Which of the following explains the meaning of "sensitive" best?
   ① getting very hot quickly
   ② being very thick
   ③ not feeling anything
   ④ feeling things strongly

5. What is the common word for the blanks?

   • Brain receives millions _____ messages every minute.
   • You should drink plenty _____ water, too.

   ① to
   ② of
   ③ into
   ④ for

6. Which characteristic is NOT right about a four-eyed fish?
   ① It has four eyes.
   ② It has two eyes.
   ③ It has four pupils.
   ④ It has eyes that are divided in half.

7. What is special about the picture that appears in retinas?
   ① It is black and white.
   ② It is upside down.
   ③ It is very dark.
   ④ It is round.

8. Choose all that are mentioned as the reasons why rabbits can hear well.
   ① Rabbits have big ears that are shaped to collect sound.
   ② Rabbits sit very still so that they can listen.
   ③ Rabbits go out at night, when it is quiet.
   ④ Rabbits can move their ears from side to side.

9. What keeps our ear canals clean?
   ① the eardrum   ② fluid in the tubes
   ③ tiny hairs and sticky wax   ④ three tiny bones

10. What is NOT right about bats?
    ① Bats have excellent hearing.
    ② Bats fly at night.
    ③ Bats make tiny clicking sounds.
    ④ Bats cannot hear the clicking sounds.

11. Which one listed the moving path of tiny piece of smell correctly?

① nostrils → the space inside your head → special hairs → brain

② nostrils → brain → the space inside your head → special hairs

③ brain → the space inside your head → special hairs → nostrils

④ brain → the space inside your head → nostrils → special hairs

12. Which body organ does NOT relate to taste?

① tongue   ② nose

③ brain   ④ ears

13. What is NOT right about the human sense of taste?

① Tongue cannot taste things on its own.

② There are taste buds all over your tongue.

③ The nose and the tongue work together.

④ When you cannot smell, you can taste very well.

14. Which of the following parts is the most sensitive to outside stimuli?

① the tips of your fingers   ② the bottoms of your feet

③ the top of your head   ④ the backs of your hands

15. Through what can blind people read and write?

① by using sign language   ② by using Braille

③ by reading lips   ④ by wearing special glasses

※ Choose the correct word(s) for each blank. (16~17)

16.
> Have you ever _____ in school when you are tired?

① is ② are
③ was ④ been

17.
> Your brain is _____ than any computer.

① powerfulest ② powerful
③ powerfully ④ more powerful

18. Choose the correct sentence.
① Sometimes this happens because a disease of.
② Sometimes this happens a disease because of.
③ Sometimes this happens because of a disease.
④ Sometimes this happens because a disease.

Sarah J. Dodd

Sarah J. Dodd is an experienced primary school teacher who resides in the UK, but has also lived and taught in Australia. She has a PhD in Science and a certificate in Creative Writing. She has published several books for children: "An Angel Anyway" (Anyway Press, 2008) the "Little Angels" series (Lion Children's Books, 2009/10), "The Lion Picture Bible" (Lion Children's Books, 2015) and "Legs: the tale of a meerkat lost and found" (Lion Children's Books, 2015). Her poetry for children has also been highly commended and published in the anthology "Let in the Stars" (Manchester Metropolitan University, 2014).

She is currently working on further picture books for the very young, and a novel for older children.

 Smart Readers Wise & Wide 2-5

My Body Is So Clever!

Written by Sarah J. Dodd
Illustrated by Sunkyong Kim

First Published in December 2015

Editorial Manager: Juyon Choi
Editors: Jiyeong Park, Kyunghee Jang
Designer: Eunhee Lee
Cover Designer: Eunhee Lee

Published and distributed by

 Happy House

Darakwon Bldg., 64-1 Jandari-ro, Mapo-gu, Seoul, Korea 04031
Tel: 82-2-736-2031(ext. 250)   Fax: 82-2-732-2037
Homepage: www.ihappyhouse.co.kr
Publisher: Kyudo Chung

ISBN: 978-89-6653-213-1 18740 / 978-89-6653-156-1 18740(set)

[Components]
• 1 Audio CD (Recording Studio: Aram)
• Answer Keys & Korean Translation: Free download at www.ihappyhouse.co.kr